Divining Bones

Sundress Publications • Knoxville, TN

Editor: Erin Elizabeth Smith
Editorial Assistants: Tierney Bailey and Laura Villareal

Special thanks to Jenna Geisinger.

Colophon: This book is set in Bell MT.

Cover Image: Kevin Hinkle

Cover Design: Kristen Ton

Book Design: Erin Elizabeth Smith

Divining Bones
Charlie Bondhus

To Hannah –

Hope you enjoy this journey
through Baba Yaga's forest!

[signature]

10·19

Acknowledgments

I'm grateful to the editors of the following journals. Many of these poems were originally published in different forms:

Assaracus: Witchcraft and Demonology *(reprint)*
Bridge Eight: One Can Never Be Sure When It Comes to Cryptozoology
Burnside Review: A First-Grade Production of *Oedipus Rex*
Chelsea Station: If you can't be a boy, be a houseboat, I am starting to
   remember Atlantis and so are you, The Hagiography of Sister
   Dottyback Devilray, Sexual Fantasies
Columbia Journal: Ablation, Bloody Mary (published as "Catoptromancy"),
   Demiurge, Demimonde, Demitasse, Demon Lover, Self-Portrait as
   Baba Yaga
Cream City Review: Study for a Flat Earth
Full Moon & Foxglove: Baba and I Klatch Over Reasons Why We Hate
   Magick (reprint)
MiPOesias: This is Baba Yaga, Baba Yaga and the Bones, Portrait of My
   Mother as Baba Yaga, and Baba Yaga's Legs
The Missouri Review: The Red Barberry
The New: Witchcraft and Demonology
Nimrod: Guilt Keeps Us Busy; Violence Makes Us Creative, Baba and I Klatch
   Over Reasons Why We Hate Magick
OCHO: A Journal of Queer Arts: Baba Yaga and the Horses, Baba Yaga Does
   Porn, Becoming Baba Yaga
Poetry: The Satyr Proffered, Sunday in the Panopticon
Split This Rock Poem of the Week: A Car, A Man, A Maraca
Tupelo Quarterly: The Octopus Jar

Table of Contents

For Coatlicue, who brought me underground.

For Baba Yaga, who met me there and taught me what I needed to know.

This is Baba Yaga

At the blue second birdsong begins,
Baba Yaga rises, old bony leg
thumpity-thumping slatted steps
to the green yard where mushrooms grow.

Dew soaks the fibular as it does
every morning, getting into the spaces
between bones, where she aches
the ache of peasant girls

and czarinas. Today a laboring
throb in her left foot;
yet she's lived enough
to understand all pains

are bearable if one knows root
and herb, the ninety-nine uses
for deer urine, which of the mushroom's
many ridges holds magic.

Baba Yaga burps, scratches her rump.
Behind her, the house turns
on two ribbed and restless
chicken legs. Bending, she begins

to gather the orange-yellow *lisichki,*
the brown-capped *beliy grib,* the maiden
pale *veshenka,* clutching a bouquet
of fungi to her breasts, the breasts

that anchor her to the earth.

The sky turns a lighter shade of blue.

This is the Book of Baba Yaga.

This is the Book of Baba Yaga.

This is not the Book of Baba Yaga.

Plans for a Doll

1) *The Prince smiled like a man with all the guns.*
2) Sitting in the wings were the following:
3) a live cat
4) a mummified cat
5) an onyx cat.
6) The custodian sketched a compass on the floor.
7) Tersely I spun the astrolabe.
8) I heard the eyes of the audience members.
9) I heard them moving inside their heads.
10) We remembered the coatroom and its intrigues.
11) The compass is a metaphor.
12) I sat at the northernmost point, drawing my legs beneath my body.
13) You described your plans for a doll that peed
14) but only if one poured water in the back of her neck.
15) That too, a metaphor.
16) Somewhere, an alarm clock's ringing.
17) The proscenium arch sustains both
18) drama
19) and
20) prediction.
21) *It so happens I'm tired of just being a man.*

Witchcraft and Demonology (I)

When I was 13, I read *The Encyclopedia of Witchcraft and Demonology* cover-to-cover.

Some of the pages were glossy as wet skin:

full-color photos of demons copulating with witches.

Asmodeus, Baphomet, Legion, Malphas.

Female bodies wrenched into postures that defied the dictates of bone.

Many-armed lovers with manifold teeth. Beautiful as saints, but meatier.

Hell seemed a place where horned lovers with a thousand cocks would treat my soul as if it were a body.

But I promised my mother to be gay, not queer.

No broomsticks, desecrated wafers,

or dancing naked under the moon.

Instead, monogamy and mortgage, friendship and four walls,

the only magic, the Catholic kind,
wine turned to blood on Sundays.

By day witches work as dental assistants
ordering the mouth's yellow-red chaos,
picking dirty talk from the teeth,
soothing gums scorched by spells,
scraping the tongue which is tired from pronouncing
the thousand Sumerian names for Satan.

What Mom Thought

When they took him away
so I could sleep, I felt
guilt in my belly like gas.
But then my head hit
the pillow and I was dreaming
of a house on chicken legs. Though I didn't know
what I was doing I said *little house,*
little house, stand with your back to the forest
and your front to me and the house did as it was told.
I climbed its steps and parted
its curtains which hung like tattered lunch meat.

Somewhere, a baby was crying. I went room
to room, opening doors which closed
behind me, the crying growing louder
then softer. I wasn't in a hurry
and was only a little annoyed
when I found myself back in the original
room which now smelled of freshly baked
bread, but when I opened the oven
there was no bread—
instead, a baby.
Mine?

When I woke up
they brought me my son
and I bore him
the way you
bear rain.

Ablation

This is what the body needs—to not be
                                        itself.

It takes some patience and I can't always do it,
but give me an hour in front of the mirror
and my chin will start to get pointy.

Recurring nightmare: I cut myself
and nothing comes out.

In all my childhood photos
my hands are folded behind my back.

Or I'm kneeling.

My limbs are necessary until the elbow.

Sometimes 0 just makes the most sense.

If you can't be a boy, be a houseboat*

My brother told me not
to be stupid
so I went outside and played in the rapids
that had appeared in our backyard.

The water churned and I was dragged
under, the currents two competing impulses
until my legs became the smooth
curve of a hull, my outstretched
arms hardened into a swan-
shaped figurehead, and I bobbed
to the surface.

I thought about mom and how
after she'd turn out the lights I'd go under
the bed and make lists in two columns like:

hammer	hand drill
boat	barracuda
boy	mule
mollusk	raspberry
cactus	cowgirl

I motored downriver, penis dragging
in the cresting wake. Large birds circled my rigging.
Kids ran along shore and yelled.

I'd never been in such a good mood, not even when I'd gone
to the circus and seen
the gator-boy with his
human eyes and filed teeth and understood that
what I wanted to be was two things
at once; it didn't matter which.

---

*The title is a line from Mai Schwartz's poem "Atelier" as it appears in the Spring 2015
North American Review.

Baba Yaga and the Horses

Horses gather
                    at the mouth
of the cave
                            where voices drift
like the feather-soft
                                    seeds crowning the dandelion a boy
holds to his
                            lips, puff with powdered sugar and
fffffffffff—the horses
                            shake dust
from fetlocks and Baba
                            Yaga crawls out,
sly, like a child
                    who needs
the bathroom
                    but wants
 to win the game
                    of hide-and-seek she's been
playing, tossing
                    her voice all afternoon
to draw   the herd from lake
                            to prairie
to forest
                    to cavern, heavy hooves crunching
pebbles, battering
                            down crabgrass, tramping dandelions
into seedless
                    stalks the boy
finds and frowns, asking
                                    where did the flower fuzz go?
Idiot child, it's clinging
                            to their muzzles, Baba Yaga mutters,
                    watching
a fine-boned foal breathe
                    wetly in the late

afternoon gray, the whites
                      at the corners of her eyes showing
as she seizes
            on the smell of two clawed
hands, a mouth
                full of iron teeth—and yellow-
eyed Baba Yaga
        rips into her.

Witchcraft and Demonology (II)

As teenagers my best friend and I tried to summon the dead
using a Ouija board and a planchette which moved
from point-to-point, plotting a response
to our uninspired questions
about what it's like to be dead.

Like the waiting room of a dentist's office:

boredom, bad chairs, Reader's Digest,
four walls and dread. But worst of all,

the end of ambiguity. Trust us, they said,
you'll miss it
when it's gone.

Swinging Doors

And then there was that weird
summer when the grill rolled

across the patio and knocked over
the garden gnome and a snake poured

from sill to sink before sliding
down the drain and at camp

I saw what I thought was my older brother kneeling
in front of another boy though I couldn't

be sure. My perception
of all boys had been off since

I'd found the changing rooms
(which used to be private)

were now wide-open so I could see
all my naked friends

with their scrubby pubic hair
and unkempt assholes which made me feel

like I knew them less than I had before
and when the counselors told my parents I seemed

"disconnected"
I said the only thing that was disconnected

were all those swinging doors
which according to campfire scuttlebutt

had been removed to make us
more like men

though when questioned about it
the counselors would claim

they'd been torn down
by pervy ghosts.

The Octopus Jar

your dreams at night will
be as strange as the jars of octopus you saw once in a fisherman's boat
under the summer moon.

-Robert Hass

1

Out past bedtime
a boy is searching rowboats
when he spies the jar,
contents twisting
like a complex dream.

2

Heavy-eyed stevedores drink brown
beer in the harbor-front tavern;

a couple who've just met
make out on the pier—
eight writhing limbs.

3

The voyeuristic cat is confident
he has eight lives left.

4

Drawn by a damp
fishy smell,
a seagull
pecks at a cracked jar.

5

The psychoanalyst stumbles
to her desk...writes:

Eight arms in a jar
indicates the secret body
with its unexplainable appetites,
its slick, snaking halls.

6

An old woman walks the moon-wet
beach, her footprints bisecting
loops some child or other
drew with a stick.

Baba Yaga and the Bones

Tonight she's ravenous
and so she waves the pestle
like a mad signalwoman
and descends,
having spied
a small, whitish heap
of dry sticks, cracked spheres,
disconnected hinges.

The smell of bone is like pheromones;
she reaches into the pile,
clutches the stiff curve
of a femur.

Thinking of meat
she runs her hands
along the bone's white arc, fingers
tensing until
snap, and
the broken bits
drop into her lap.

She gathers them, raises them to her lips,
slurps the red and yellow filling,
filling her mouth with the long dead,
imagining she can detect beneath the decay
the jumpy taste of children,
something she craves
but has never had.

I am starting to remember Atlantis and so are you[*]

most of all the residents, who weren't
so much *tapered, with hair like underwater*
fire as
bodiless embodied,
jellyfish, trans-
lucent, trans-
parent, dichogamous (*sequential*
hermaphrodites), skins *pearl-*
rainbow or oil-rainbow depending
on light, cruising crenellated
columns, not mermaids/men, but more
cthonic, cnidarian, amphibian, though don't mistake
this for an andro-
gynous origin
story, genderqueer pre-
lapsaria, *we did not come*
from the sea yet somehow we remember it,
you said, then wondered (wandered?)
about the webbing
between your fingers while I
drew an ouro-
boros at your lovely, fishy feet.

---

[*]The title is three lines from CA Conrad's poem "stArting to stArt heAling" as it
appears in *Troubling the Line: Trans and Genderqueer Poetry and Poetics* (2013).

Witchcraft and Demonology (III)

The devil Baphomet,

born of the Greek *baphe* and *metous*. Baptism and wisdom.

When I was 15, I scribbled in notebooks crude drawings

of the goat-headed androgyne,

crafting, with the help of my Latin I textbook, invocations

to a being who sat with one arm raised, one arm lowered

as if to tell mankind—as Jesus did—it's through degradation

that we raise ourselves.

On the upraised arm, the word *SOLVE*—separate.

On the down-pointing one, *COAGULA*—join together.

While my parents were at work I lit candles, sacrificed an astral goat,
read my homemade incantations

to the demon with female breasts, leathery testicles.

Bloody Mary

light a candle, chant
at the mirror, and you'll see
her in you: the old murderess,
the bloodthirsty abortionist.

After the thirteenth incantation it began

at my chin and spread
across mouth, jaw, and cheeks,
until my lower face was hers.

11 years old I already knew
the joys of being home alone; of leaving
my bedroom door open as I pushed my pubescent cock
and balls up inside, imagining myself
as something else.

When I touched my new hard
lips I thought about Mom,
whose disapproval was stronger than any witchcraft.

But it was already too late.
When I turned on the light
my face had become
sexless as an egg.

Baba Yaga and the Child

On a village sidewalk lumbering Baba Yaga trips,
startling pigeons into the dumpling hot air.

Her nostrils grow
hot with a delicious smell, filling her
throat as the flap that separates
esophagus from stomach
cracks open. The child is small, sharp-faced
with limbs like a doll
made of sticks. Nothing Russian about it;
her first American child smells
of new clothes and breakfast cereal.

Heaped on the sidewalk the two
are close as gristle and bone.
The child's beak-thin elbow cuts
a concavity in Baba Yaga's womb,
creating a sharp, strumming pain,
like a small foot
thumping the softness
beneath the ribs. *The second it-child,*
Baba Yaga thinks somewhat tenderly,
to cause this discomfort, like and unlike
the hunger throbbing her heavy,
upended body, a pile
of loosened earth where rootless things
sometimes grow.

Giggling, it disentangles itself
as Baba Yaga clutches her
gut, feeling (truth
or dyspepsia?)
the living and dead
children seething
like gastric juices,

stewing her
from the neck up
as she extends one
feeble claw after
the brat
who's already
skipped off.

Witchcraft and Demonology (IV)

Three-faced Asmodeus,
patron of lust
and its queering—
one head a lamb, another a bull,
the third: a man breathing fire.

Demon son of King David,
I promised you my cock
for one weekend
with your powers.

Then, every straight guy
wanted to fuck me:
a grimy, zit-faced boy
with mismatched eyes
and a creepy smile.

A First-Grade Production of *Oedipus Rex*

Creon stutters "anarchy"
and trips on his chiton,

knocking over a Corinthian
column made of fruit boxes.

The smell of half-rotted
honeydew spills from the stained flaps

as the non-union argonauts
smoke cigarettes by the loading

dock and Miss Meropa recalls
the prophecy

the boy who ended
up playing Tiresias made during

second period. Costumed in six-year-old
certainty, dire predictions flew

from his mouth like harpies. Neither
the school nurse nor the class healer

could restore his sight
and that's how we got

here, the greasepaint chorus
shrieking and chattering while

it stumbles left to right, still
landing, as rehearsed,

in the correct spots.
Just like fate, Jocaste

mutters, tightening
the rope around

her waist. *No matter how*
torn the map or

how many forests,
rivers, and deserts missing

or mislabeled we still arrive
in our predetermined places

all because somewhere else the gods
left a trio of grim

sisters the busy work of spinning,
measuring, and cutting.

Offstage Oedipus stands,
his mother's bed

sheet twisted around his sapling
shoulders, waiting for his cue,

watching it all unfold
with eyes hollow as cored fruit.

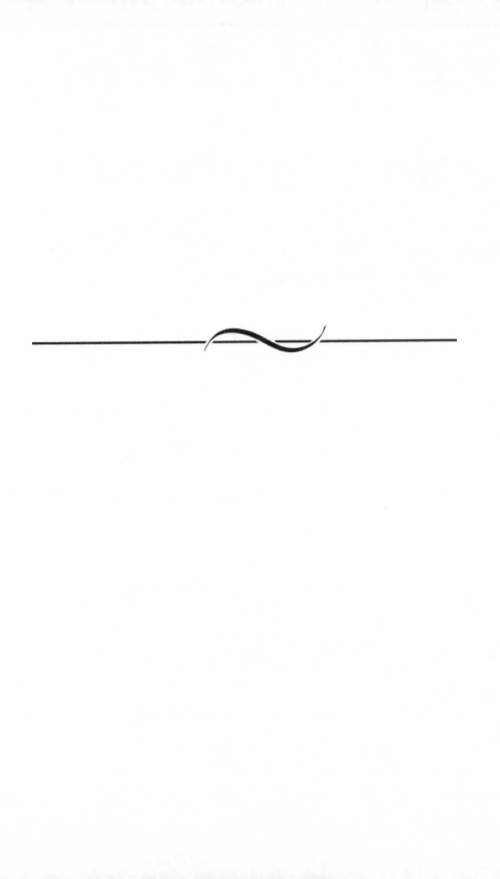

Demiurge, Demimonde, Demitasse

When women first appeared
in the world, they were declared
self-created and thus "of suspect virtue."
Yet still they came
as they were, every night gathering
on the terrace to drink small white
cups of strong black coffee which some say
was what enabled them to fly.

Where they flew was anybody's guess.
People prognosticated. Hell
was most common; eldritch
forests a close second, women being known
for their love of all things tree.

We might've speculated
until the sun went out but then one
broke ranks, talked to the press,
gave a two-hour exclusive—

*What you've gleaned from medieval
woodcuts is entirely true,* she said. *We flew to the bald, flat top
of a mountain untouched by any hand, even God's. Yes
there was naked dancing, the desecration of sacred objects,
lesbian inseminations, recreational abortions. Many of us wore men's
clothes; some cut their hair short and flexed their thick arms.
When the devil came we lined up to kiss his furry rump, an act
that briefly granted us powers beyond those we already enjoyed—
the gift of perfect sight, for example.
We saw it was not God who created the world, but
the devil, whose original job was demiurge. Once you know
where you come from nothing's really the same. But still we returned*

*the next day to husbands, wives, and children. We took up
our forklifts and diaper bags as if we were beasts*

who had been given a now-expired reprieve from commerce.
To this day, we do not forget that we're two parts
infernal, one part divine, she finished
and sat back, fingering a string of smooth waxy pearls.

The Satyr Proffered

these grapes of stone were being proffered, friend.
       -John Berryman

grapes, rough-touched and round, stone-
carved, to be squeezed into the fundaments
of rock wine. She imagines it would be cold,
not sought for its smoothness,
and likely full of grit
if not refined with care.

The satyr laughs carelessly
for one caught in stone.
The cracked edges of his mouth spill grit
as he leers after the loss of his fundaments
which fall along the smooth,
cold

torso plane, exhibiting immaculate coolness
at this literal loss of face. Carefully
she strokes his head, as if smoothing
the fetlocks handcrafted from stone.
Her affection is unforced, a fundamental
attraction to those beautiful, gritty

things made lovely by decay, his gritted
teeth so much more interesting than the gallery's cold
geometrics, which appear fundamental
but fail to consider the careless
chaos spinning at the stone
center of all smooth

creations. And those grapes! Their unsmooth
surface mirrors the messy passion flushing the grit-
dusted cheek, the hideous mouth of crumbling stone.
What heat from the Dionysian's cold,

brittle fruit! The obliteration of all care
if she could only perform the fundamental

act of eating. She thinks about wilderness, fun, mental
liberation, dancing her soles smooth,
pleasure as pervasive as care
is now, her feet a frenzied blur on the gritty
forest floor, shaking and pummeling out the cold
as she prances over starlit stones.

She does not care who sees her as she grips the stone
grapes, feels the smooth, crumbing cold
enter her hand, fingers embracing a thing more fundamental than earth,
        bone, grit.

The Hagiography of Sister Dottyback Devilray

In the second year of my novitiate, they found me floating in the supine position above the altar in the fish chapel.

All around were disembodied slit eyes, which twitched and darted.

They were, someone said, *the eyes of sexually excited reptiles.*

Some of the onlookers fainted;
many made the sign of the fishhook;
a few sang shanties.

Yet still the eyes swarmed, like candiru around chumming.

Everyone thought they would devour me.

So many times I had felt like a sparrow on the verge of flight.

But then the eyes fell prostrate,
tamed, like obedient dogs,
and disappeared.

My tits made it necessary to be stern, but not too stern;
my penis allowed me a certain puckishness.

For days afterwards, the chapel reeked of lizard guano.

No one ever saw them again, except me,
for whom they were ubiquitous
as those red and blue birds that lived in the belfry
and sang the hymns Sister Aloysius taught them.

And in the same way that Sister A was eventually named

La Patronesse de los Pájaros

I came to be known as

La Virgen de los Flying Lizards.

Baba Yaga Does Porn

First on set she's taken
in by the lights—whiter than the skin
she thinks she wished for as a girl.

But has she ever been a girl? Baba Yaga
could never be a child's name and yet
she can't recall ever being Anya or Vasilisa.

She unravels her headscarf,
lets fly ropes of hair, braided,
which slap against her backside.

In the mirror her body
is an old downy pear with too many rot spots.
Still, she's told there are men who will pay
for such things. Tapping pockmarked

fingers on a doughy thigh, Baba Yaga tries
to imagine such men, men who reject
beauty's slick uncertainties for the reliable
inertia of a wrinkled breast and a pale teat,
men who find beauty threatening
in a way a hobbled bone leg isn't.

No, Baba Yaga decides, thoughtfully hefting
her gut, she was never beautiful,
nor was she ever consistent, pleasing
in the way ugly girls ought to be,
and though she thinks there was a time she wished herself

fair as bone,

she can't be sure of her own story anymore.

She glances around the set:

a king-sized bed, hotel furniture,
inoffensive tchotchkes,
a room where anyone could live,
but who would choose to?

She dresses and departs, flies

high above the San Fernando Valley,
pausing at 30,000 feet—an unseen, low-hanging star.
As always, it's the distance

that makes her invisible, the distance
and the light.

Sunday in the Panopticon

I was sitting in Old Town Square
with tourists and birds and I was reading
Foucault, how *he who is subjected*
to a field of visibility becomes
the principle of his own subjection
and all around me the beautiful
Slovakian boys moved through the first
day of spring like perennially
visible inmates in the opening credits
of a prison porno. The sun reflected off
the glass and my table was an inscrutable
tower of light from which I peered, invisibly,
at the swan-graceful boys who seemed to skirr
across the stones, traveling, it seemed, to something
vaguely ridiculous and charmingly anachronistic:
cufflink shopping, or brunch with the duchess.
The coffee had made me jittery and I was beginning
to sweat from both sun and desire. I considered
moving to the outer edge of the circled tables so the boys
could see me as I could see them but then the 600 year-old
orloj sounded the hour and the twelve apostles
and skeletal death spun around and I was afraid
to leave my tower. I didn't want to be visible
in the way those small dancing figures were visible and,
as much as I wanted a handsome companion, I feared my foot
getting caught in a sewer grate or my spoon
falling from my saucer and clattering on the pavement,
startling the birds into a ruckus. An errant ball
of sweat fell from my chin and onto the page. I looked
down to where it had landed on the word *reciprocal*
which made me think how looking is always reducible to twos—
two eyes, two parties, two possible outcomes, and how
those who watch from the panopticon's black pupil may,
in any case, not even exist.

Becoming Baba Yaga

I was born an old woman,
I mutter through lather
as I scratch away the beginnings
of a beard, each stroke bringing me
a hair closer to alignment
with the female divine
curled and kicking inside, while I glare
at the little snub nose which belies the long,
crooked phantom pressing my skin
like an erection in the underwear I buy a size too small.

My dreams are full of chicken legs.
My thighs tingle for the swish
and stroke of a checkered peasant
skirt. Invisible handwoven blouses girdle
my imaginary breasts. I tug at my boy-short
hair and think about raspberry-colored headscarves.

There is no other way
to say this: I was meant to be a wise
and powerful Russian witch
rather than an unimpressive man,

a truth that makes me ambivalent
about the pretty young women
who come seeking transformation,
asking me to shave away the fat
a child left, straighten a nose
crooked as a kidney bean, plump
up breasts that are like the hard, rounded
nubs of an old cook's pestle.

Like any witch I serve
the vanities of all who can afford
my fee, helping those who hate

their bodies in ways different
from how I hate mine. I study

the college photos they bring
of glamorous, uncomplicated youth,
remembering an old, lost book
and the engravings in which I recognized
myself—a fierce, bestial woman
as necessary as bone and just as unseen
in a world whose first language is skin.

Sometimes when I'm finger-deep
in a body I think about the way beauty slithers
through the tunneled centuries,
collecting and sloughing trappings as it goes,
and I know my inherent self,
though not beautiful,
is timeless in the way of snakes,
storms, and ancient forests,
and if I were to turn scalpel and curette
on myself, out would pour a great and silent river
of clear water
from whose banks would emerge
wild things
unknown to beauty... here, here;
grip my hand and you'll see it too—
wet fire;
living skulls;
a house that walks;
a male crone;
Baba Yaga birthing herself.

Witchcraft and Demonology (V)

Once I dated a man whose room was a perfect square.

I lay on the bed and
mentally subdivided the
room into nine smaller
squares while he fucked
me. I wanted to kiss him
once in each subdivision
so our affections would
radiate equidistantly

from the center and
creep up the corners.
I was going to marry
him, make it square.

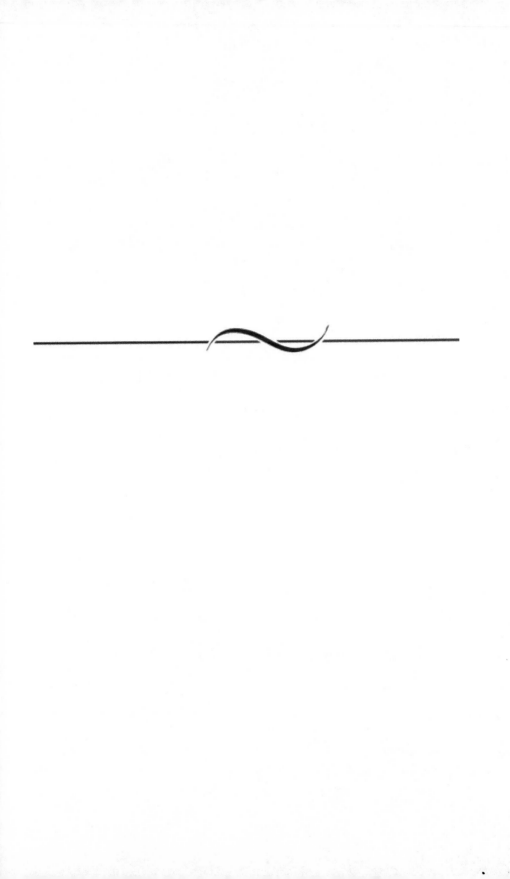

Demon Lover

When we first met I dubbed you my demon lover, which was a mistake,
because I had no basis for it other than your leather
jacket and the persistent smell of struck matches. Still I convinced

myself that some night you'd tear
your human face like wrapping paper
and show me and our friends just how sexy

you were with horns and a tail and though *that*
never happened there was the time you took me to bed
and showed me the things that rippled just beneath your shoulder

blades like trapped birds beating a cloth-draped
cage and when I said they looked like the twitching
stems of wings you said you'd been born with a genetic

defect which had given you malformed appendages
resembling blighted angel wings which took
many surgeries to remove. I asked you how large

the wings had been and you said *Large enough*
to be noticeable beneath my shirt but not
what you'd call "Marquez-sized" and when I said

That's hot you told me to fuck off.
But ten minutes later we were naked
on the bed and though your body didn't feel

any different than it had before knowing I was being fucked
by someone who was part-guy part-angel
made all the difference in the world.

Witchcraft and Demonology (VI)

I used to be married.

On my wedding day the compass spun and refused to settle on any one
point.

As if preparing for guests, the spirits in our house bustled,
flinging pulses which upset the crockery.
My leather tingled on the hanger.

The Justice of the Peace extracted promises from the narrow, painful
spaces between our teeth.

We bled for weeks afterwards, and the blood stained the bristles of our
toothbrushes.

Every time we spoke, it was as if our mouths were full of raspberries.

Guilt Keeps Us Busy; Violence Makes Us Creative

I asked you to scrape the bathroom
and you painted a Turkish
bath scene on our bedroom ceiling. You wanted
a gun rack to store your hunting rifles
which were sprawled across the kitchen table
like centerfolds and I built a jungle gym
for the little boy who lives at the end
of the cul-de-sac.

We tried talking it through but power
tools interrupted, the circular
saws ululating in their grooves, heralding the arrival of Jesus
Christ who said there's no greater miracle
than the cordless drill. *You see, boys,* he explained
God IS electricity. I spent centuries in wine
since it was a place to sit
still (alcohol being a poor
conductor) but then came the lightbulb
and for the first time in 2000 years I was visible, useful.

Sometimes we see the boy
biking in the neighborhood and it leads us down
that unproductive path of whether
we should've had children and is it too late now?

Guilt keeps us busy; violence makes us creative.

Whenever we feel like denying
the Lord, I flip
the switch and you
shoot out the light.

Portrait of My Mother as Baba Yaga

You laugh when I tell you how I'd hide
beneath the covers where my stuffed animals were rats
with human faces and mom
was the bogeywoman
grabbing with strange fingers. *A game*

like being tickled to screaming. I'd thrash in the hot
dark until the sheets were soaked in my juices
and Mom was a cackling chef,
furloughed from the polite society of my father,
playing with her food.

Sexual Fantasies

1.

Visiting the erotic frescoes of Pompeii, we watch Priapus

lean back and gesture at his impossible member
and the spreading cracks.

It sounds like the set-up to a joke
but I'm serious as a temple
when I say

this does nothing for me.

2.

On a dare I shave my eyebrows and commit
to the clean alien look, scraping away
pubes, pits, legs, head.

My genitals are an arctic plane.

3.

On a Chelsea rooftop the rich queer
artist pours concrete over my bare

legs. The rented mariachis
play "Cielito Lindo"
and the world gets harder.

4.

I'm Bonnie Tyler and you
make love to me onstage—

halfway through the second
chorus of "Faster than the Speed
of Night" and I don't stop singing.

It gets on YouTube

but my parents don't recognize me
because I'm Bonnie Tyler
and my hair is feathered.

Study for a Flat Earth

The Alien Cathouse is a Nevada brothel
where the girls dress in glowing

latex, big black contact
lenses, pulling sad-eyed

men with jaws
like donkeys. One grumbled

lines from Hart Crane—"A jest falls
from the speechless caravan"—and I thought

about the planet and my need
to invent proverbs—"Blessed are

the lighthouse keepers, for theirs is the beam that cuts
the flat earth," or "you would hate it in the desert

where the saguaro's yellow
flowers bloom only at night."

Nevada makes me think of streptomycin,
and when we left Brooklyn

all I remembered was a book
on a shelf and orange tabbies

on a fire escape.
The title was *Study for a Flat Earth*

and I wanted very much to take it
with me but the voice of God—common

to deserts—spoke of "the night
sky's indigenous smell" and how

virtue in its highest form resembles "lights
circling a UFO's perimeter." Later,

when she removed her mask
I saw that, like me, she was neither

beautiful nor plain:
the kind of lady who,

if pressed, I would have to describe as
"A most handsome woman."

A Car, A Man, A Maraca

At the mirror I heft
elbows, belly, cock,
say *hematocrit—44.3; hemoglobin—15.2;*
neutrophils—62; monocytes—5.

You've stopped
reading and seem to be counting
the buds on the campanula.

Carbon dioxide—25, I say, *high end*
of normal; testosterone—297, low end
of normal, though I'd rather topical
cream than shots.

Outside our window a car passes;
rounded light lassoes
my legs, hogties me,
like in an old cowboy movie.

I remember one where the evil
gringo prospector is smuggling a priceless
Zapotec fertility statue
inside what appears to be nothing
more than a broken maraca and in the end
when the incorruptible *vaquero* returns the statue
to the priest they discover that it's been battered
and chipped to the point of androgyny, and I think
the title was *A Car, A Man, A Maraca*, but
when I tell you, you laugh and say
that's a palindrome and I respond *my potassium,*
chloride, and calcium levels are all normal
and you, thinking I didn't understand, explain
it can be read either way and I say, *yes.*

Baba and I Klatch Over Reasons Why We Hate Magick

The smell.

It only works if someone else asks for it.

Teenage girls in black nail polish.

It's the only thing that separates me from the animals.

After I cast a love spell mosquitos follow me for days.

Candles get expensive.

I also play the guitar but you didn't know about that did you?

Men think it's sexy   at first.

Never knowing whether I'm being asked for a hex or sex.

Concerns about sustainability. A finite resource, like water or time?

It's always a hex.

What would happen if big pharma caught on?

At the end of the day it's just another form of housekeeping.

It never works on me.

One Can Never Be Sure When It Comes to Cryptozoology

I found a Bakhtak
beneath the abelia bush
in our code violation garden.

His left ear was folded like a page;
his right looked like it had been chewed
by one of the jackals who roved our complex,

looking for remains.
I wondered if this Bakhtak was clockwork,
placed by the condo board to spook

us into compliance.
Our garden had long been a sharp bone
for the Carriage Greens' establishment party—

all those *bright and buggy flowers
in princess colors.*
I was going to see if the Bakhtak had a door

in its breast, but then it rolled over and
swung a small, vole-like claw. I remembered
my mythology—the Bakhtak as *bringer of nightmares*—

and considered disposal by fire,
but then the little guy cooed—
really, it cooed—

so I dropped the cigarette lighter and picked
a few banyan leaves, swaddling it until
only its old man head was visible.

It made loud mewling sounds
that seemed part-cat, part-flute

as I carried it into the condo and laid it on the kitchen floor.

It was hungry, yet it turned its nose up at the milk,
roughage, and raw meat I took out of the refrigerator,
even refusing my offering of whisky in a bottle cap.

I thought maybe it subsisted on fear,
negativity (You were still at work).
One can never be sure when it comes to cryptozoology.

90% Lean

You call it a perfect night for red meat,
and now nothing, nothing
can be right,
not even the kitchen window
collecting the snow,
not the snow itself

(and all through the house
I hear it piling up).

The heater heaves and the freezer
is full of death. I can't

think about the cows any more
than I can think about the pigs,
or the lamb, or the duck, or the goose.

You know I've been pawing
the gristle
like a raccoon
at a trashcan.

I saw you watching me as I knelt
in the refrigerator's snow-gold glow.

Loin, rib, rack, shank.

You have not spoken
to me since.

Portrait of My Husband as Baba Yaga's Hut

I didn't see it before, but my husband's asshole
is the entrance to Baba Yaga's hut.

It smells of dead leaves, unswept corners, the stray cats
who gather in its shadows to speculate
about the weird old woman
who gave them language to speculate.

His floorboards groan when I enter.
A slight harrumph from the stove—Baba Yaga
is tending the fire, tapping her bony heel.

She's kinder than the fables suggest,
offering food—bread, milk in a bowl,
an egg—as she dusts her
collection of skulls.

Baba Yaga burps, scratches her rump, reaches beneath
her skirt and tugs out a baby (*no, a doll*)
with knobby joints, thick fingers,
indeterminate genitalia.

I tickle it and it pees on my hand.

I understand one day it must grow large
and grapple with obscure emotions.

When I open my eyes I've become a woman
drying sticks in her apron.

Crawling out from between my husband's
matted chicken legs, I look back

but Baba Yaga has already turned out the light
and drawn the curtains.

Red Barberry

When you left me I was tending
the red barberries

which bordered
the neighbor's property

in an uneven row, like my two
bodies, the future one having

found ways to occupy roughly
the same space as my present,

so when you looked
at me I was blurry,

flickering, a double
image, something resembling

a man, but
hybrid. This was further complicated

by my semi-transparency—
something to do with future

and present selves occurring
in the same temporality—

so it became difficult to tell
me from me from barberry,

my three-and-a-half legs red
and sharp, my belly a burning

bush, my hips like sticks. You said
you could never love

a half-man and I said you
could never deal with red barberry

because it attracts ticks
and increases soil acidity

and has been identified
by the Council on Plant Hybridity

as an evasive species.

Baba Yaga's Legs

She glances down
        at her glowing leg, musing
as she sometimes does,
        what this mortal mark
was meant to signify.

Could it be death? Everything
        seems to remind her of that—
the corpse-cold earth,
        the coffin-wood trees,
the song of the birds
        sounding like the soul
flying from flesh.

She turns to her other leg,
        the living one,
thick-veined
        and curdled
with cellulose.

A breeze ruffles
        the black hairs which grow
between the liver spots
        and she cringes, totters,
grasps the bony leg
        which is smooth
and whitish-gold,
        like the polished backside
of an expensive hand mirror.

It strikes her death
        is what's best in her—
and most beautiful.

Witchcraft and Demonology (VII)

And Jesus asked him saying, *What is thy name?*

And he answered, saying *My name is Legion; for we are many.*

In the original Greek, the word is *chora*, the space

between the teeth and the tongue, the demon and the god, the witch and his familiar.

Self-Portrait as Baba Yaga

Sundays I go down to the Hungarian
deli on the Lower East Side where
I can get away with eating children
if I'm sly about it, slipping them
into the goulash when no one's looking.

Later I cruise Coney Island
in my mortar and pestle, but
only the elderly Soviet emigres
and granny fetishists pay attention.

These days I cast queer spells and
burn myself at the stake for the crowds,
offering nickel love
potions to the lovelorn at 33rd and 7th.

I have a tortoiseshell cat who catches mice and speaks
Polish and a tortoiseshell comb that turns
into a city when it's thrown on the ground.

When out-of-town children
ask my gender, I tell them
I'm a witch.

Witchcraft and Demonology (VIII)

I used to be married
until I asked him

Why must we always be crossing? Isn't the bridge enough?

We had known no magic but the Catholic kind,
wine turned into blood on Sunday.

The Justice of the Peace extracted promises
from the narrow, painful spaces between our teeth.

Every time we spoke we fancied our mouths full of galaxies.

I went to the dentist and he found a planet beneath my gums.

The End

It was spring, late afternoon, and I was coming home from school. My books were under my arm and my heart was like the sun with the moon in front of it. I walked an unfamiliar path, a shortcut through the woods. Birds cried mating calls. Green tips pierced the dirt. A few sticky flowers spread their flushed petals.

Do I need to tell you that no matter which way I tried, I seemed to go deeper? Do I need to tell you that the birds got quieter, the forest darker? That the branches which cut across my path became a stranger's fingers? Well you probably know the next part too—the house with the chicken legs, turning and turning, like the engine of the forest. I remembered the stories and knew my part. I planted my feet and said "Little house, little house, stand with your back to the woods and your front to me," and the house did as it was told.

Baba Yaga was there of course, and she was naked. When she saw me, she spread her legs to reveal books, neatly shelved. They were without titles and every spine was as black as the eye's pupil. I looked into her eyes and it was clear what she wanted me to do, so I did it.

The book was hot and heavy as a kettle of soup. I peeled back the cover and tried to read what was printed there, but the words bobbed around like boiling vegetables so that the meaning kept changing. I looked up and she was laughing at me. She laughed so hard that she split in half.

Both halves continued to laugh as I ran out the door, huffing and puffing all the way home where my mother was waiting and

Notes

The "Baba Yaga" poems – Baba Yaga is a witch/goddess from Russian folklore who lives in the forest in a hut that's constantly turning on a pair of chicken legs. Known for her earthy, occult power, she's often cast as an antagonist, but can be a helper too—a guide who assists the protagonist on their quest. She's usually depicted as a crone, with one leg made entirely of bone. Unlike the western European witch who flies on a broom, Baba Yaga flies in a mortar and pestle. Similar to Hansel and Gretel's witch, she allegedly eats children, but I have yet to read a folktale in which she actually succeeds. I'm indebted to *Baba Yaga: The Wild Witch of the East in Russian Fairy Tales*, trans. Sibelan Forrester (UP Mississippi, 2013).

"Plans for a Doll" begins with a line from Martín Espada's poem "Something Escapes the Bonfire," *The Republic of Poetry*. (W.W. Norton, 2006) and ends with a line from Pablo Neruda's "Walking Around," *Pablo Neruda: Five Decades, a Selection (Poems, 1925-1970)* trans. Ben Belitt (Grove Press, 1974).

"Witchcraft and Demonology" — most of the demons referred to are catalogued in *The Goetia: The Lesser Key of Solomon*, the earliest version of which dates back to the 17th century. The exception is "Legion," who appears in 3 of the 4 Gospels—Mark 5:9, Luke 8:30, and most notably, Matthew 8:28-34. The Gergesenes—alternately, the Gadarenes—was the name of the land where Jesus encountered the man beset by "Legion."

"The Octopus Jar" – the epigraph is from Robert Hass's poem "Spring Rain" as it appears in *Human Wishes* (Ecco, 1990).

"The Satyr Proffered" – the epigraph is from John Berryman's "Dream Song 6," from *The Dream Songs* (FSG, 2014).

"Sunday in the Panopticon" – the panopticon is a theoretical building complex which Jeremy Bentham first imagined and Michel Foucault later used as a metaphor in *Discipline and Punish*—from which the italicized quote is taken. The panopticon, usually imagined as a prison, is comprised of a round outer building which encloses a large courtyard with a round tower in the middle. Prisoners occupy the outer building and are constantly visible to the guards who occupy the tower. However, the tower and its windows are constructed in such a way that the prisoners cannot see into the tower. The theory is that because they can never know for sure whether they're being watched, the prisoners must always assume they are, and will self-regulate accordingly. The "600 year-old / *orloj*" is the Prague Astronomical Clock in Old Town Square.

"Study for a Flat Earth"— "a jest falls from the speechless caravan" is from *The Bridge*.

"One Can Never Be Sure When It Comes to Cryptozoology" – a bakhtak is an Iranian demon. Fuseli's painting *The Nightmare* depicts one.

Thank You

Many thanks to the many people who read and commented on this manuscript in its many (many, many) iterations, including Kris Bigalk, John Bonanni, Steven Cordova, RG Evans, Ian Haight, Kevin Hinkle, Charles Jensen, Dean Kostos, Stephen Mills, Michael Montlack, William Reichard, and Carol Rosenfeld.

Thank you to Erin and the entire team at Sundress for supporting this project.

Thank you always and forever to Kevin, for his undying love and support.

And finally, my deepest gratitude to Coatlicue and Baba Yaga, for their difficult wisdom.

About the Author

Charlie Bondhus is the author of *All the Heat We Could Carry*, winner of the Thom Gunn Award for Gay Poetry. His work has appeared in *Poetry, The Missouri Review, Columbia Journal, Hayden's Ferry Review, Bellevue Literary Review, Nimrod,* and *Copper Nickel.* He has received fellowships from the Virginia Center for Creative Arts, the Sundress Academy for the Arts, and the Hawthornden Castle International Retreat for Writers. He is associate professor of English at Raritan Valley Community College (NJ). More at charliebondhus.com.

Other Sundress Titles

Phantom Tongue
Steven Sanchez
$15

Citizens of the Mausoleum
Rodney Gomez
$15

Either Way, You're Done
Stephanie McCarley Dugger
$15

Before Isadore
Shannon Elizabeth Hardwick
$15

Big Thicket Blues
Natalie Giarratano
$15

At Whatever Front
Les Kay
$15

No More Milk
Karen Craigo
$15

Theater of Parts

M. Mack
$15

What Will Keep Us Alive
Kristin LaTour
$14

The Minor Territories
Danielle Sellers
$15

Actual Miles
Jim Warner
$15

Hands That Break and Scar
Sarah A. Chavez
$15

They Were Bears
Sarah Marcus
$15

Babbage's Dream
Neil Aitken
$15

Posada: Offerings of Witness and Refuge
Xochitl Julisa Bermejo
$15

Suites for the Modern Dancer
Jill Khoury
$15

Every Love Story is an Apocalypse Story
Donna Vorreyer
$15

Ha Ha Ha Thump
Amorak Huey
$14

CPSIA information can be obtained
at www.ICGtesting.com
Printed in the USA
BVHW030003100919
558014BV00002B/36/P

9 781939 675743